PRONOUNCED / WORKABLE

PRONOUNCED / WORKABLE

Candace de Taeye

Mansfield Press

Library and Archives Canada Cataloguing in Publication

Title: Pronounced, workable / Candace de Taeye.
Names: De Taeye, Candace, 1985- author.
Description: Poems.
Identifiers: Canadiana 20220447713 | ISBN 9781771262644 (softcover)
Classification: LCC PS8607.E786 P76 2022 | DDC C811/.6—dc23

Typesetting and design: Denis De Klerck
Cover Art: Candace de Taeye
Edited for the press: Jim Johnstone

The publication of *Pronounced / Workable* has been generously supported by
the Canada Council for the Arts and the Ontario Arts Council.

Mansfield Press Inc.
25 Mansfield Avenue, Toronto, Ontario, Canada M6J 2A9
Publisher: Denis De Klerck
www.mansfieldpress.net

CONTENTS

9   Preface to Basic Life Support Standards

Protocol

13 Pronounced / Workable
14 10-8
16 10-7
18 Anecdotal
20 Out of Service
21 Work-Wife
22 The Lay-Hero Archetype and the Public Access Defibrillator
24 Pantoum
25 10-9
26 "B" is for Basic Life Support
28 Cimex Lectularius
29 Cerebrovascular Accident
32 Destination

Document

35 Leisure World
36 Subpoena
38 Major Incident Field Guide
39 Barrier Method
40 Google Translate App History
43 "Hotel Sierra"
44 Personal Effects

Memento Mori

47 Dead Doppelgänger
48 Un-barren Newly
49 Thanksgiving
52 Heart Opening
53 Death Naïve
55 Contemporary Psychopomp
57 Obits i, ii

Gravidy

61 BLS Standards- Obstetrics
62 Cannonball
64 Waiver
65 Heart Opening II
66 Work Hardening
69 BLS Standards- Pediatric General Assessment
70 Driver

Accumulation

75 Accumulation

Unprecedented

85 Chronology
  Isolation Rooms
86   1 March Break
87   2 Exposure
88   3 Not All Things Being Equinox
89   4 Speakeasy
90   5 Hesitancy
91   6 Role Identity
92   7 CareMongering-TO
93   8 Bottle Half-Empty
94   9 Apnea
95   10 Community Medicine
96   11 To the Poets
97   12 No Visitors
98   13 Inevitability
99   14 To the Beloved

100 It's Hard Not to Slam a Fist on The Table When the Finish
    Line Keeps Lurching Further Ahead - or- Third Wave
106 Omicron Grand Finale

110 **Disclaimer**
111 **Notes**
115 **Acknowledgements**

PREFACE TO BASIC LIFE SUPPORT STANDARDS

Can you give me something? *In field practice*
diagnosis is of secondary importance.

Intended to maximally protect patients from receiving
inappropriate care. To describe the Rorschach blots of blood

on backboards? *And service providers from being subjected*
to always remember that resuscitation is one part lullaby.

Provide verbal and where deemed appropriate, tactile
comfort and reassurance. That you have mistaken my hunger

for sadness. *All paramedics can now be assessed*
using the same objective criteria, like the resourcefulness of vitals

written on clementine peel. The experienced ones
perfecting their skills in postures of defeat.

Protocol

PRONOUNCED / WORKABLE

As an adjective
clear, evident,

As an adjective
capable of producing
the desired result

as a noun
as a body
declare or announce
formally
the doctor has

as a noun
as a body
Vital Signs Absent
but not
obviously so

as a verb

Return of Spontaneous
Circulation

make the sound
of a word
"dead" /ded/

lub dub
"save"
viable, achievable

In the correct or a
particular way

work and able
a verb and adjective

articulate, vocalize
myself
from the Latin
nuntius
messenger

in the present
tense
strong, practical
a wide base
blue collar

10-8

In service
on air
en route

'The Knowledge'   supplemented by a screen

speed limits prescribed under this section do not apply to

      two waspy women jogging
      "I just registered for the death race"

plan to align
with the single corner housing
the elevator that descends to track level

nod to Intersectionationalities

the ghost of little Malta

          is a bakery

          the first step in gentrification?

          Pape and Danforth
          Dundas and Spadina
          Greenwood and Gerrard
                Geocode 09063 D5

where the paramedic is
unable to locate the address

proceeding through red lights
a complete stop before
slowly pull forward
when it is safe to do so
blocking the first lane of traffic
but stopping short of the next lane
repeat the above point
until the intersection has been cleared

On scene
off air

into the building envelopes
the real 'Doors Open Toronto'

    the bath houses, after-hours clubs, shelters in church
basements, money counting rooms deep beneath Bay St.,
greased undercarriages of streetcars, locked dementia
wings, sally ports and prisons, the Bridal Path, sweatshops,
apartments hoarded to the ceiling or ones with children
sleeping on nothing at all

response time

        the time measured from the time notice is
received to the earlier of the following

        any type of defibrillation

take a pulse / anatomical landmark

the xiphoid process
where the ribs come together
heel of hand two fingers above that
point /stack hands one on top of the
other/ begin compressions

antecubital fossa /needle stick

        (g) be free from all communicable diseases

the HIV clinic of the hospital hidden on a middle floor at

the end of a hall/ at the end of a hall/ around a corner.

patient destination and selection procedures: sure
if any part of the hospital bears your name.

what a

Bundle of His

ANECDOTAL

Framing of extraordinary occlusions
extrications, arrhythmias.

Precordial thump

save.

The pedagogues of improvisation and
aubergines swallowed by...

We know better
than
"What's the worst you've ever seen?"

Our stories

a currency

and resonance.
Here's one;

"I don't want mommy to be dead.
I want her to make me chicken."

Women birth sons and then they disappear.

The wound is transitional.

A body before and then
with scar.
Wounds are liminal   where medics exist.

Women especially   compare this before
and after best.

Shape-shifters we're fluid and leaking

residue.   Locard's theory.

My work is
                                  of the body?
Women's poetry always
                                  of the body?

I'm an ambulance driver   not unlike

1976?
Bed /oxygen/ blanket.
Mother, Jugs & Speed

A ghost among them.
Muscle repetitive memory   strain

In the garage permutations

920...944...850...960...818...845...901...

                a locker holds your space.

OUT OF SERVICE

A 45 Station Valentine's Glosa

Sic transit gloria mundi.
This city is full of ghosts
visual meteorological conditions
and restlessness.

How doth the busy bee?
Women's change room.
20:05 Eastern Daylight Time
card swipe below – Lieu? or

dum vivamus vivamus.
Wile E. Coyote in aviators
eternal tagline. Heli tail and
main rotor system.

I stay my enemy
youth. (buzz) Departed
over a farmer's field.
Fatally injured not Ornge

Personal attitudes towards death influence sleeping or working hours. How they communicate then a buffet/thrift store adventure. Skinny and sturdy bitch sizes. A qualitative study of trash-pandas and Baker Bots. We fawned over those lawyer hands. Themes generated inductively. You can make reasonable taco meat from walnuts? Everyone will cry at some point. Fantastical, the support mechanisms a logistical nightmare. Montreal cackle date if you're not in extremis, fresh figs, squee. Banh Mi Boys consistent with the gender demographics (24% female). Baking something for C-shift in an urban service more positive about slogging, I trust your judgment, book the flight transcriptions. Field notes were analyzed downtown. Calls on the Danforth, that's too far east, FML, AEMCA, B.Sc., MScCH. What type of support? I gagged; you have excellent stories like the rabbit head in the fridge. Depends burrata or bone marrow? Excessing, the Frenchies do it too. See you tomorrow. Lived experiences such as that one, single truffle, stopped us, props. From now on everyone hits the floor. Order of the good-death versus songbird eating deer, and oh, the Love Plate.

Can affect the family's grief process, breaking people by proxy. Reasonable, alpha dog isn't teaching anymore, so your stethoscope is safe. Difficult to switch from a clinical to support role. No more spite lifting. Samosas or flat white? Skills are easier to teach, too many feels soft and chewy. It had to be scraped off with steel wool. Poorly with her practical skills, it involved coat hangers obviously. The bread with a soul, addition of the termination of resuscitation. Andes vista breaks, happy talking blood hands, dual roles and book smart. Now nesting or 3 banana epaulettes. Health Nut smoothie reminisce the deaths that are poignant, informal, or much too much. Code 5, sigh, and eating Thobor's croissants. Yass- in every scenario.

THE LAY-HERO ARCHETYPE AND THE PUBLIC ACCESS DEFIBRILLATOR

i. Being Called to Act

She clasps the lion's jaws, quickly scans the room for
Hermes, or any other contemporary psychopomp. Is
someone wielding a caduceus? Re-conceptualized
as simple, safe in a public space. A culturally consistent
protagonist lay-rescuer. Transcribes verbatim an event
"He" "is on exhibit too" "as he is dying" "as we watch him"
Utterances, pauses and paralanguage Jungian.
An important determinant, the role
of mouth-to-mouth is deemphasized.
Witness(ing) their collapse
is disturbing. Self-doubt and unanswered questions.
Rigorous psychological sequelae. Constructivist
grounded theory. Seizing control of an earthly situation.

ii. Taking Action

Galvanizing compressions. A case of seekers versus
victim-heroes. Not firefighters or fairy godmother
donors. Rich deep descriptions of the colour blue.
Cyanosis, convulsions, incontinence. Strengthen
trustworthiness. Iteratively agonal respirations are
misinterpreted. Fixate on victim's face. "[quiet voice] dying"
Generally, wields a special weapon or supernatural aid.
Enter Automated External Defibrillator. Admittedly
*"I was really guessing at what the machine
wanted me to do"*

iii. Making Sense of the Experience

Apotheosis or the journey and the un-healable wound.
Framed as moral responsibility. In half the cases
the victim ultimately died. Descent into a kind of hell
"there are corpses" ..."and emotion" "strong emotion"
and one matures greatly. Define the optimum balance
between accessibility and realism. Return of spontaneous
circulation. Frame perfusion as an infinity symbol. Reluctance at the
label, returns to their desk and posture correcting chair anew.

PANTOUM

"It's fine, I'm fine, everything is fine."
In the middle of microwaving your lunch again
It's two am, there's still seven hours to go
It's really about the journey from innocence to experience.

Caught in the middle of microwaving lunch again
After a certain hour every 3rd patient is Beetlejuice.
It's really about the journey from experience to empathy
Neutral chaos, typecast as the Trickster.

After a certain hour every 3rd patient is Beetlejuice.
And the city leaves little room for characters marginalized
in neutral chaos, typecast as the Tricksters.
"Nah, he'll start breathing again any minute",

society leaves little room for characters marginalized.
It's a surprising lack of freedom few acknowledge.
He'll start breathing again any minute, probably.
Hastily rolling bodies over the hospital threshold.

Surprising amount of privilege few acknowledge,
being a white woman in your mid-thirties. Almost always
enthusiastically invited over the threshold.
I still refuse to wear a vest, trust people are inherently good.

White woman in my mid-thirties, non-threatening,
but I've been punched in the face, bitten and groped.
Still, I refuse to wear a vest, trust that people are good.
Didn't Mr. Rogers say 'look for the helpers'?

Lets not forget being punched in the face, bitten, groped.
It's only two am, there's seven hours to go.
Didn't Mr. Rogers say 'look for the helpers'?
It's fine, I'm fine, everything is fine

10-9

En-route with patience

in which a siren is continuously sounding
and from which intermittent flashes
or red light are visible in all directions

yelling at the old man for his name
his name at least

                                    wages for tenderness

Wolf-Parkinson-White
Syndrome and the impulses
can travel through extra pathways
a short cut
through the heart
circular pathways
too quickly

I prefer to take Church south rather than Yonge, less traffic
and lights, the ride is smoother especially over those fading
rainbow crosswalks, past the bar where my then boyfriend
kissed my uncle's neck, a right onto Shuter, jockey for a spot,
lean in and run up the ramp, an invariably dramatic entrance
beside the clean injection kits.

"B" IS FOR BASIC LIFE SUPPORT

Still choosing
   accessibility over authority

            opposite Advanced
life support is graded

     role identities arranged
                         I'll write
                 my microcosm too:
        rural childhood, first love, new motherhood

by the way the nurse always looks   to your
shoulder first
                hierarchically within the self

tenets   of symbolic iterationism

same pants
same local
as the garbage crews

the mildly call us   social scripts   Nicholas Cage
perhaps
                  Bringing Out The Dead

they will remember the most expeditious
     the customer service piece about takeout hamburgers
                   -signed Deputy Chief

or, that I rarely pluck my mustache

incongruence
           increases
               proof of relevant experience

note: the complexity and careful
synchronization
not a legacy
but delegated acts

authorized by a doctor I've met once

*"Imagine your sense of self as a pie chart. How big a slice does being a
paramedic get, and why?"*

a whole   lived
body   of work

  four dimensional; caregiving, thrill seeking, capacity, duty

the medical-legal disadvantage
I'm capable of preforming   often simultaneously

                    profane and polite

quit before you break
but then it doesn't register as moving   to Guelph

                    when will you work there?

*Everything we do
is about leaving our patients*

CIMEX LECTULARIUS

Bedbugs the size of a pinhead, flax or apple seed, complete with a hypodermic knife penis. Isabella Rossellini shouts 'Seduce Me!' in spandex but everyone else is ashamed. Hiding their linens. Coats wrapped tight vestigial wing nubs. Rape-y bastards, traumatically inseminating each other right in the gut. You need to steam them as if trying to get a good froth from skim milk. Kafka into book spine. Diatomaceous earth arcs apartment doors. Optimistic protection, like garlic for other sexier hematophages. Females rarely emit their alarm pheromone, unlike the topped gluttonous misread males. Sultry harborage smells of rotten raspberries. Rostrum into your nape, thighs, even that little pocket behind your knee. Studies hypothesize resisting may be higher than the cost of consent. Bean leaves Balkan magic Velcro. Thank DDT for fifty years without that phantom itch. Bed, bath and beyond the bald eagle omelets.

CEREBROVASCULAR ACCIDENT

Dosages slip, contraindication.

The entry code- four corners
one two three four star
street number
or was it the year?

A year is a long time.

New onset

drift.

Unilateral words
droop slurred.

Inappropriate:
"I've got to prune the tables in the backyard."

Within 3.5 hours of a clearly

not

sugar <3mmol.

Seizure
onset uncorrected.

Coma scale   ill.

Resolving Michigan J Frogs still go designated.

To get there: head north on University that turns into Avenue and
past 1,2,3 of the richest retirement homes in the city. Turn east onto
Eglinton, past the intersection where the Ferrari hit the pedestrian,
then jumped into the bank on the southeast corner. Turn north onto
Bayview, the lit up 24 hour Metro, where someone nearly lost an eye.
Up the hill past the Whole Foods on the left, on your right complex
continuing care children. Then turn right into the driveway, stay right,

past the cancer center, park just past the research building where they cremate the lab mice into tidy plumes of white smoke. Entry code for the ambulance door is the street address of ___, then pound. Triage is through to the right. Hit the blue button at waist level. The acute stroke bed is 14 Green.

Spontaneous unlearning.

Engineered as a not unpleasant
                    apoptosis.

Popcorn fanned across the lawn, my great
grandmother walking
                    me home from kindergarten.

She never spoke
again. I can't remember
her first name.

                                        Acceptance

          of half clocks, plates, bodies in neutral
          letters indiscernible.

Airway
Breathing
Circulation

Onset
P....?
Quality
Radiation
Severity
Time.
                                        A year is not very long.

The alphabet and
teaching him to hold the pencil.

"to R-

Love great fairy Uncle R-"

Have you seen my dragon?
I will look at the bookstall, my dragon loves to read.
Count   9 orange books
... 12 pigeons
...19 green lights.

Hippocampus or surrounding cortices.

Not encoded verbally
lost accessibility. Recall
as children age

you will never be loved this much again.

Versus, his anterograde
fragmented
episodically forwards.

DESTINATION

Arrival

      or the hospital formerly known as Grace

or alternately,
      here, a 13-year-old boy
      didn't want to be forgotten. Now,
      three-meter-tall letters spell out his name.

'When you have a wall that's facing a direct route
that everyone passes it's a conversation'
      ANSER's Mysterious Date as part of the landscape

            we all want a little permanence

re-learning the men
named arrhythmias, bone breaks or physiology's that
lie within us.
            that's immortality

offload you beside
the daily John and Jane Does
occupying the hall-beds

Document

LEISURE WORLD

Secured Floor |Memory Word List| Week of August 13, 2018

holiday	Toronto	Islington	dog
you	Ossington	like	GO
ugly	no	envy	caviar
Yonge	owing	gentle	relax
easy	Georgia	love	X-mas
young	always	elephant	cake
glory	sons	train	
yes	good	Tagalog	
sweet	don't		

SUBPOENA

"What do you remember?"

His silhouette reclined.
Blue-green powder residue
cheek peck. Two plain-clothes,
and then rain.

I did not see this
from my bedroom window.
Palpate an entry and exit

Executed.
They pulled up real close.

"How close? 30 ft. or was it 100 ft.?"

Well before police

"There is no other
record of this sedan."

behind us watching.
Matching descriptions

(Did you insert a racial imaginary here?)

of the car. Disappeared
when we didn't

work him.

"spell...   C-R-E-P-I-T-U-S.
        ...for the record."
                        I

wet brick grinding
bone on bone.

While briefly
lifting up his head
Once, he too had newborn
scalp scent.

".....from the asphalt."

Muse or meuse?

Don't appropriate.

Draw a map of the incident area.
Name it. Geographical atrophy
and humbling acts. We bore witness.
Spadina's igneous boulder, several James.
All roles defined within this document.
Heron and blood. Huron and Bloor
landmarks the Unknown Student.
We are treating people. We are all treaty
people. Triage report an oral history. The job
offer conditional on hearing and lung capacity.
Tuberculosis. He replied again "Pokaroo"
and his friend said "Hakuna Matata"
not December but a pharaoh in a joker t-shirt.
That was 3 years ago and today he got
absorbed into the body politic.
"I can smell your pussy from here!"
Consider wind direction and that the sky got bigger.
The rock, the size of his head, lifted from the border.
Facial bones unanchored continents "I exist
in human form." Reconcile silence as a concept.
We didn't need more time, just coffee.
Environmental influences. My partner stares
at a garden center flyer. Hosta's colonizing backyards.
Terra Nullius. Initial resources on scene. Free
prior and informed consent. Offer "You were
sleeping." Direct walking wounded
to the treatment area. "No but my buddy here,
has chest pain." Access to amenities.
Soon she starts to breathe again, asks
"...but were there any other Indians around me?"

BARRIER METHOD

purple to blue
impermeable

separates
when I wear

which is not
always, not often

previously latex
of trees

so a page
lies between

language barrier
and chords

body cues
posture

bullet vest
a bound chest

divisions
response areas

across the city
our borders

你对什么过敏吗? — Do you have any allergies?

你有服用什么药物吗？ — Do you take any medications?

당신의 생일은 언제입니까? — When is your birthday?

உங்கள் முழுப் பெயரையும் உச்சரிக்க முடியுமா? — Can you spell out your full name?

你为什么叫救护车? — Why did you call for the ambulance?

Tvoja kći nas je nazvala da je zabrinuta. — Your daughter called us she was worried.

Nije se čula s tobom od četvrtka. — She had not heard from you since Thursday

你有什么痛苦吗? — Do you have any pain?

¿Algún dolor de pecho? — Any chest pain?

ای آی ام ش بت داشته ای — Have you had a fever?

¿Le han dicho alguna vez que tiene arritmia? — Have you ever been told you have an arrythmia?

¿Un latido cardíaco irregular? — An irregular heart beat?

Потому что вы принимаете антикоагулянты. — Because you are on blood thinners.

Milyen fájdalomra szedi a morfiumot? — What pain does he take the morphine for?

그와 마지막으로 대화한 시간은? — What time did you last talk to him?

그녀가 오늘 넘어졌나요? — Did she fall today?

这是她平时走路的样子吗？ — Is that how she usually walks?

Cuando aparcamos en el hospital. — When we park at the hospital

Pondré más pegatinas en tu pecho. — I will put more stickers on your chest

Para mirar tu corazón. — To look at your heart.

你的血糖太高了. — Your blood sugar is too high.

혈당이 너무 낮았습니다.   Your blood sugar was too low.

우리는 당신에게 설탕을 재울 바늘을 주었습니다.   We gave you a needle to bring up your sugar.

그녀는 전에 이 문제를 겪은 적이 있습니까?   Has she ever had this problem before?

Bạn có bất tỉnh không? "Mất điện"?   Did you lose consciousness? "blackout"?

Van pacemakered?   Do you have a pacemaker?

며칠 동안 그녀의 소변이 아팠습니까?   How many days has her urine been painful?

سعی کنید تنفس خود را کند کنید.   Try to slow your breathing down.

Máshol fáj?   Do you have pain anywhere else?

الان باید برم بیا روی تخت سپس شما را در پتو می پیچیم   We have to go now. Come to the bed. Then we will wrap you in blankets.

我们有她的药。   We have her medications.

أحضر أوراق الهجرة وجواز السفر.   Bring your immigration papers and passport.

உங்களிடம் பயணக் காப்பீடு உள்ளதா?   Do you have travel insurance?

我们要去儿童医院。 市中心。   We are going to a hospital for children. Downtown.

医院会有翻译。 他们会更好地解释这一点   There will be a translator at the hospital. They will explain this better.

¿Tiene ganas de vomitar?   Does he feel like vomiting?

ما می توانیم صبر کنیم تا پسرت به اینجا برسد   We can wait for your son to get here.

بعد از آن با هم صحبت خواهیم کرد   Then we'll talk.

خیلی طولانی نخواهد شد   It won't be too long.

我们必须等待与护士交谈。   We have to wait to talk to the nurse.

این فقط تا زمانی است که اتاق شما تمیز شود. This is just until your room is cleaned.

Nem fogják megtagadni tőle a gondoskodást. They will not refuse him care.

Még akkor is, ha nem tud fizetni. Even if he cannot pay.

我们只需要注册。 那么我们有一个房间给你。 We just have to get registered. Then we have a room for you.

你今天吃东西了吗？ Have you eaten anything today?

Amikor visszatér a regisztrációhoz. When you go back to registration.

Mutasd meg nekik, hogy a papír segíthet. Show them that paper it may help.

당신의 남편은 몇 시간 전에 사망했습니다. Your husband died many hours ago.

죄송합니다. I'm so sorry.

'HOTEL SIERRA'

and 'Staging' are the two new radio phrases we will introduce.

Confirm they can speak, be properly
groomed and dressed.
The purpose is to ensure that _____
provide prompt and effective
care. The purpose is mutually satisfactory
relations between the city and its employees.
Identify obvious hazards, routes of
entry and exit. Consider making verbal
contact by lobby intercom.
When choosing to delay
provision of service. Its use must be
understood. Danger exists, or uncertainty
out of the vehicle, in proximity to persons.
_____ are reminded of their responsibility
hair must be neat and of a natural colour.
Situations that pose a risk or threat
these exclude _____ from the right to refuse.
Fingernails trimmed and maintain political neutrality.
Withdraw, if possible or practical.
Only the top button of the shirt may be left unbuttoned.
Consider metabolic causes of combative behaviour
affords unchallenged access to many restricted areas.
If their work refusal would endanger the
Health & Safety
of (an)other person. Judgment based
only on specific available information
and must follow the direction of management.

PERSONAL EFFECTS

(items transported to hospital with patients)

- a pair of lavender crocs.
- a raspberry beret and purse concealing only napkins and coffee creamers.
- a rice maker.
- an old curmudgeonly Akita dog and a moderately bloodied medium size Jack Russell Terrier.
- a mobile IV pole stolen from a hospital (the patient was still attached.)
- the 'ring finger' of a left hand, complete with 2 slightly mangled rings, and 20cm long remnant of tendon.
- a small domestic rabbit in a small stroller.
- the most delicious smelling charbroiled hamburger (the patient was an unreliable historian and could not tell us where he obtained it.)
- a $6000 bicycle.
- a foam 'LARPing' sword.
- a 1.5m tall fiddlehead fig tree.
- A school backpack full of stolen steaks.
- 200 condoms, 15 individual packets of lube, 2 seasons of 'The Chappelle Show' on DVD, a dime bag of meth, and 17cm hunting knife tied up in a black tube sock.

Memento Mori

DEAD DOPPELGÄNGER

Only once have I cut sleeves from dead weight
arms and revealed my own neck down reflection. Ashen

face unfamiliar but same torso or so, nipples, breasts,
hips, umbilical dimple. Mirror chest compressions.

UN-BARREN NEWLY

Urine soaked addition sign equals
pelvic ultra sound
    brief interval of three and not two
indication: threatened abortion
    the sun pink-orange of a candled egg morning of
comparison: none
    no brie, no prosciutto, no sashimi
anechoic cystic structure
    cautiously optimistic
likely represents a gestational sac
    nesting disbelief
no fetal pole identified
    dramatic classically trained buskers on violin
no yolk sac is seen
    the tiny salamander in a bubble was dead
cervix appears closed
    expired prior to resembling a salamander
right ovary is within normal limits
    the opposite however had been ecstatic
hypoechoic structure likely
    his womb ached with seahorse wishes
representing a corpus luteum cyst
    harder to convey news to the home-front
non-visualization
    amidst nausea and corkscrew cramps
anembryonic pregnancy
    I was disappointed not devastated
or blighted ovum
    conception was at least possible

THANKSGIVING

I'm breaking the wishbone
snapping a breast bone
feeling crepitus at the sternum

You're not breathing or wishing.
Keeping both halves buried
chest deep - almost to heart.

Lime green scribble ambles
across the monitor. An earthworm
newly exposed to sun,

or vectors
of electrical current
through cardiac muscle.

Your heart at this point
resembles a bowl
of Jell-O trembling.

Raspberry or orange being
the only two flavours my
Great Grandmother used

for her standby salad ring.
A Thanksgiving staple served
with the bird not dessert. She died

last September. So, I worked the holiday
because we had a funeral instead
of a good meal. Tiny Sandwiches

don't get you into Valhalla.
Hollandaise and truffles
please. Skimp on the box.

My uncle was there. He turns
loved ones into keepsakes
with the push of a button and 870'C

Unrecognizable is the key.
Like the animals in the midsections
of the crustless canapés.

We all just keep stealing carbon,
making it our own. North Americans
are 60% corn if you really get down to it.

Thanksgiving immortalizing
expatriates harvest. Unrecognizable
corn as syrup, oil, and gravy

thickeners. Feed the cow ate,
who is beef now. Hungry
worms will eat Grandma Maxwell

and use her carbon, from corn
and otherwise. Writhing about when
tilled up in the field on a sunny day

until they lie still and flat. Then we
will call it asystole- and call the doctor.
Leaving you still and flat.

I will ask your wife for a grocery
bag. The one she toted the cereal
and ground beef home with.

I'll collect the packaging
and disposables strewn about the
dining room from our attempt.

Then your wife, glassy eyed -
She will insist I eat.
She made too much.

HEART OPENING

Resuscitative thoracotomy a ceremony
more colloquially known as 'cracking
the chest'. Threshold on every medic's
voyeur list from the 4th to 5th intercostal
space. Absolute acuity as ribs are retracted
watch the high-priest lay hands on.
Bypassing the electrical impedance
of skin and bone. Regardless
Bee Gees 'Staying Alive' is optimum
compression tempo, or cardiac
tamponade. Like sex, most people
can only be vigorous two minutes
at a time. What right do we have
loathing the multifactorial
suffering of chronicity so much?
Our parasympathetic ganglia lie
close to the spine. Weight bear in service.

DEATH NAÏVE

What if we measured care by deep
observation, not empathy?
My every day will be their
worst, they try to impress
upon at the interview. I forget.

No labour/ no bread.
Food's the most ephemeral
so I feed the dead lady's
cat while I scan her bookshelf.
Clive Cussler? The sturdy medic weeps

over the mouthfeel; handmade
tortelli from *Famiglia Baldassarre*.
Do others aim to insulate themselves
from suffering, or is it really
from death? Must we all be

contaminated though? Commiserate
as the PSW becomes unemployed
once the death certificate gets signed.
I propose, as in love, degrees of
affectation. Lover, platonic, to mere

acquaintance deaths. If most abstain
from all but the intimate
does it skew the concept? Or, am I silted?
The young and early mourning get
pariah-ed. Indicators of uncommon

loss. The grad student's suicide note
on the screen, not paper. Who'll return
the helium tank to the balloon store?
We judge the practical aspects. Each medic
could offer a personal preference.

We think about it a lot. More than
one might consider political affiliation.
Even if we never plan on running
for office, one or two a year
from this service always do.

CONTEMPORARY PSYCHOPOMP

Actual survivability of an out of hospital cardiac arrest is
v slim

this is
opposite of journalism

                                resuscitation as ritual
strangers in uniform
re: authority   secular yet   reverent act

galvanizing
compressions

sweat, produce strange tools, divine some lime green
scribble, break a rib, open the throat, grunt, inflate the
chest, induce contractions with a walloping biphasic jolt

                                parallels to birthing
experience
               liminal   peri-death
                             lullaby

who's present matters
               some families want to watch up close, most prefer
to stand
               at the doorway
others,
out of earshot   *(pauses and paralanguage)*

   what dying actually looks like

an observant   whippoorwill   accommodates

you can't CPR

on a mattress
the neo-ritual concludes

use the word
"dead" /*ded*/

"the beginning of the long dash followed by 10
seconds of silence"

OBITS

i

Shirley (Grandma Smith)
                        - died May 29th 2018.
Over six feet of towering matriarch. Biceps
of Rosie the Riveter. No shrinking violet,
but a giant Redwood that teetered precipitously
the last couple years. Neuropathy of a famously
uncompliant diabetic. Always had the best
cereal selection, but never sugar-coated
her thoughts. No one dared to touch
the thermostat set to 'Arctic' between the years
1983- 2016. She was a mother, a worker
and a bit of a rebel. She will be fondly remembered
anytime I encounter Schweppes Diet Ginger ale
televised tennis, or an entire shelf
of Harlequin Romance.

ii

Papa Gartner
                        - died Sept 6, 2021.
Decided he'd rather not enquire
about how reversible the stroke was.
No left limbs—fine. Unable to swallow
—mildly problematic. Refused transport
IV's or G-tube. I wonder if the skin-hungry
ladies at the dog park know yet? Always
had a way with women. European style.
Turtlenecks, black socks and sandals. The smell
of summer sausage. Longevity secured by a pack
a day and three fingers of C.C. Outlived two wives.
Entrepreneur of decorative wrought iron
who refused to teach me to weld.

Gravidy

BLS STANDARDS -OBSTETRICS

Be sensitive to maternal
    cravings on night shifts, even outside our response area.
Fears for the unborn child
    by strangers while you shrug them into the ambulance.
If discussed be as comforting and reassuring as possible
    that this bump is a water balloon of safety, built on lifting.
Do not give false hope.
    of ever being Stay-At-Home or part-time. Dad could
interpret the findings in light of a lack of acuity
    from a brain marinating in 30x the progesterone.
Anatomic changes of pregnancy lead to uniform
    malfunctions, progress to stretch-top tactical pants.
Complications, fisticuffs with the no longer unconscious
    overdose in the elevator.
The preferred compression technique was an abdominal
    sucker punch by the middle age cerebral bleed.
Two thumbs on the lower third of the sternum with fingers
    tearing into that croissant, cradling cappuccino.
Encircling the chest and supporting the back.
    Promoted off the road at your discretion, or it's
been determined that birth is imminent.

CANNONBALL

The perpetual taste of toads and pennies
had long since left my mouth, leaving no
reason to doubt the ultrasound tech.

First, I had dared you into existence
by booking that flight to Nepal.
Then you evolved, in the Pokémon sense,
past a salamander to a gummy bear.

The size of an adzuki bean. Flax seed sized heart
the second ultrasound showed to be consistently
not beating.

I knew it was a you, zygote, blastocyst,
embryo, weeks before you became a plus sign.
I was rehearsed this time. Welcoming, I
had chosen flight cancellation insurance.

Then you became an elephant in the womb,
not in size, just taboo. It's been three
weeks since you were labeled non-viable.

Disrupted by a space, a tear,
a subchorionic hematoma.
Its potential cause: lifting very premature babies
in their incubated 300lb boxes, repeatedly.

Last night I opened a bottle of wine
labeled 'Cannonball' on the cork's side
a tiny boy silhouette, knees held to chest.

The wine that filled our glasses spilled
on the table cloth. It had nothing on the spectacular
mess you made of my pants today
while walking through the grocery store.

WAIVER

a document or thing a (birth)story produced by a person in the course of review the lost bearing (now) and privilege pain tolerance had been central my identity relinquishment (requested at 8 centimeters) my what a strong back you have! -the anesthesiologist

two fist counter pressure on either side of my sacrum the forearm bearing down the chain ink of oxytocin Steve has a big emotion sleeve but how much synthetic titration did I need to overcome the apathy (post-dates) feel hard enough to push my parenthesis polyhydramnios translates into generous greenhouse (extra legroom) she was glad she had rolled up her sleeves this custodian tapped the keg lets plan a VBAC

-ation fair whether permitting the wishes determination or compliance maternal record I tell everyone I copped out struck out in a manner that does not obliterate the record I had not prepared reasonably for the circumstances I was now willing to disappoint these women (but he was tolerating it so well) for once I decided not to solely to prove that I could my vexatious request on their faces and good spirits willing to assume the responsibility of making a decision betrayed by involuntary pushing she shall preform on her own the functions described

determination of incapacity was just supposed to be a trial (I had believed I was stronger than most women) she called me an ambulance driver I still bought her croissants the paint is flaking in the shower soaking the tape over the cut section insignificant uterus involuting check box voiding check mom indicates readiness for discharge check serosanguineous lochia is appropriate check breast on demand

HEART OPENING II

Tracheal deviation.
Revel and weep, life is so good
tragedy must be due.

Clinical considerations, if no obvious
external signs of dearness
and apathy. One's galvanized
and paradoxical movement.

"Will I grow up to be cruel?"
This tension pneumothorax
smothered by occlusive dressing.

In service, the pharmacology
of forgetting, better yet, disassociation
rather than a hyperressonance.

A hypothesis-
is there an inverse relationship
between pain
tolerance and empathy?

Just imagine that everyone
was your mother once
or fish pose, then foamy bleeding.
Anaphylaxis, practice, practice.

WORK HARDENING

Growth

or

spiral

hardening ?

Skeletal muscle

excavate the steel toe boots, work

shirts and pants. Test zip in that postnatal stray cat paunch.

Chest press, squats, self-doubt happens. Refresh indications, dosages, trauma assessments.

Dead lifts, myofibrils, sarcomeres and study materials happen. Protocols, pathophysiology, an infant and a toddler

and spouse back home. Collective agreement, grievances, seniority. Push-ups, bicep curls, implied versus informed consent. Engorgement like wet cement hardens. And death, death happens. Meals in glass Anchor containers happen.

Re-watching the video of the baby gasping in distress happens. Stethoscope, belt, new podcasts for the commute. Dementia, hesitation and hindsight happens. Shoulder shrug, front raise, clean and press hardens, new hires and triage nurses, aid to capacity, cracking ribs, patching the base hospital physician or coroner and the cupric smell of blood happens.

Isolation precautions, indignities, egos and agonal respirations happen. Not sleeping beside your own infant several nights in a row hardens. Spiral staircases, basement apartments and white privilege happens. Weeping cellulitis legs, entry codes, fentanyl and the frozen metal of a stretcher in winter happens. The smell of overflowing ashtrays or lunch coolers wafting overripe bananas or kielbasa. Antibiotic resistant super-bugs. Seventeen-year-old quadriplegics requesting you turn that song on the radio up happens.

Language barriers happen, as well as skin-flakes, bedbugs and needle stick incidents. Sarcasm, sympathy and repetitive strain injuries happen. Rooming houses, shelters and suffering. Potholes, sheet slides and the occasional use of a stair-chair. Cold coffee, chemotherapy and Colles fractures happen. An alarm set for 4:45 am, or alternately 2:30 pm, tricep push-up and extensions, leg presses and crunches. Unprovoked police brutality happens. Miscarriages, septal wall defects, dusky babies and 300lb incubators harden. An ECG then bypassing closer hospitals to go directly to the cath lab happens. Malignant growth, flukes, and falling asleep at the wheel happens. Gunshot wounds, hangings, jumpers, seclusion, isolation and loneliness happens. Chronic pain, malingering unconsciousness, the six degrees of separation, lividity, decomposition, struggle and tenderness happens.

The red certification numbers on the top of a provincial DNR, palliative care and hospice happen. Strep. A, Hoyer lifts and lock-boxes happen. Sideways motorcycles illuminated by streetlights happen. 24hr coffee, 3am dinner, predictability, projection, sameness and aftertaste happen. Dips, pull-ups and side plank harden. Knocking on the last door at the end of the hallway, or the wrong door, or the grey of the last hour before dawn happens. Being absent for the last family dinner with grandma, or your son's 3rd Christmas morning happens. Students vomiting gin and tonic at you, shitting in their nylons happens. Cockroaches, stale urine, restlessness and incredulity happen. Choosing a favourite of the six siren settings happens. Foxglove/ Digoxin, the gelatin of ruptured globes, a little tuft of grass crowning a compound tib/fib, or the smell of overheated brake pads happens. Being bitten, groped, or punched in the face happens. Having a weapon drawn on you happens. Getting home just in time to catch the tail end of pancakes and maple syrup with your children happens. Bariatric stretchers, methamphetamine, rape, being too new to the country for OHIP, and the hot sticky unmoving air of August happen. Incorporating the overhead call tones into your dream that was about being at work anyway happens. Being the highest medical authority, a refusal, forgiveness, sympathy and empathy, empathy happens.

BLS STANDARDS – PEDIATRIC GENERAL ASSESSMENT

Handle the child gently
 microcosms of potential lack muscle tone.
En-route: prepare for vomiting in all cases
 toddlers are apex disease vectors.
Excessive drooling
 atypically rabies, again though, cherubic disease vectors.
Ask parents if they think responses are normal.
 We are not normal. Most of us have forgotten how to
use play techniques as outlined.

 Unfathomable tragedy exists. So do minor boo-boos
Use judgment to balance the parents need for action with
requirements.

DRIVERS

For the children's hospital   a dedicated   ambulance

    Relieving our medical authority

gift:
a sustainable pace
for nearly broken and very tired.   Read: I had enough

                         seniority.

trade-off:
an alarming amount of

                    infant
               near- mortality.
    Hope. Yes, hope is essential.

      The children's hospice is surprisingly close to here.

How much more desensitized could we get?
      (My partner whisper-sings lullabies to his
      little daughter while I drive us two hours
      away from book-off)

      Maybe time for therapy?

    or
    was I always?
          Not a job   for most.

  Do poets emote   or observe?
      I've never claimed to be   one.

I enjoy long drives through cottage country, even with sirens
on. Look, quaint two-story hospitals.

                              Once upon a time
                                        I wanted to be
a funeral director.

"This is fine,
 I'm fine, everything is fine"

                         My partner and I smirk,
                         bleary eyed at 3 am.

He listens to podcasts at 1.5x speed   or
                         baseball games on the am station.

His wife is due   any day now.
Mine long ago   weaned.
                             Of course, tragedy can happen
                             anytime.

We bring children
from Orangeville, Midland, Peterborough, Cobourg.

Funnel them downtown.
Specialists   and the only 24hour Starbucks in the city.

The babies tucked snug
in humid terrariums.
Rushed away from   their mothers.
                              a gentle wrenching.

I facilitate well composed
first family pics   on their phones.

         Mom's hand
                         in the tiny round door.
Actually, icepacks
on newborns
still wrecks me.   The science being sound though

no point-of-care
decisions burden   my shoulders.
I'm free to

calm.
Hold a soother.
let 'em grasp my gloved finger
and dole out some sugar.
Rock the 300lb incubator
into a bassinet.

Almost all of them fall asleep
while I drive.

Accumulation

ACCUMULATION

On the floor for days. Right at the front door
unable to reach anyone. A guest uninvited.

Outdoors, the world thaws. Kafka's on the windowsill;
we pop out the screen, make sand of the shingles.

Afterwards, we watch meteors and the neighbours.
The family you rented from, distraught that we left

you hanging in the closet. Discharged, waiting
for a ride home, the hospital bed refills.

Belt around your neck, jeans yanked up.
Juice down my chin, nectar sweet, half

of the worm receded in the peach. In the shower,
your hand still on your penis. Ecstatic knee buckle?

Unnatural neck angulation. Crown to shoulder blade.
Outside the seams of my shirt, noticed only after

your grandparents leave. Your shirt pulls
up, showing the crests of your hips and two neat

entry wounds. Then rain, a merlot stream left.
Caught in the sudden deluge, I see you

only for an instant before you lose hold. Down
the drain, eight legs disappearing. Standing

at the corner of a busy intersection. A Miss Carry
in the coffee cup, tucked in brown paper towel.

I rewrap it. Dressed in black, an abrupt jaywalk
stopping. Tossed aside by the minivan, your pink

bra cut off, left behind on the ambulance bench.
Your chitinous little thwack as exoskeleton hits

windshield, now a pale green splotch on the horizon
line. A tickle, a cough, a cough that sounds wrong.

The tear around the tumor, now your blood pools
around my knees. Holding hands, we find the calf.

The sound of Rice Krispies wells up, maggots ripple
under skin, then spill out into June. You ribs and spine

show through. A too hot mid-morning. Prompted by
heavy breathing one tent over, a drum circle

tempo matches. One side, the left, cavity down, thin
legs and dainty quail frame. Tedious meat, other half

mirrors beside. Then a book falls over the webcam lens
the moment I realize I'm broadcast. Extended family

watches the CPR overseas. Mid-treadmill with the TV
too loud. Adolescent son, starting compressions.

"Here let me" I offer. A ring of rosy hued crustaceans
transected. Antennas hoist up a lotus chip. Black eyes,

beady. Japanese tapas. Holding your hands, then feet.
Each shorn off on the subway tracks. White powder

sweeps up the blood and a wire basket of pieces.
We move onto the floor, then into bed again.

I tuck you in, still adorned with defib pads. You
always look more comfortable then. Ashore, away

from the cottage. Hours later, find the ticks buried
neck deep in our thighs. Traction gently and their heads

stay on. Only 16, I had thought you looked 25.
You slipped trying to scale the balcony. Caught

in petty theft, broken neck concealed. Also 16,
an explosive dam bursts inside you. You were

walking towards your mother in the kitchen.
Hot sandy back road, limbs tangle with leather

seats. A familiar car slows. We never knew
if you'd seen us. You fell asleep. Now

I'm dragging you out of the car. Hot blood
to my elbows, an errant post met you halfway.

Snatching up white umbrellas by one leg. Trucks
fill. Many die before they are reduced to breasts

or drumsticks. Lost hiding from the daily thousands
who retrace their route. Confused, but now frozen

beside the expressway. Your address blocks away.
Discovered in the early morning. Milk already

put to cereal. Stiff and tawny. I'll carry you out
after the kettle whistles. Fault cat. Pulling

the noodles, a birds nest congeals—out
of your throat. I had to pause, step away and vomit

in your kitchen sink. Escalating from a little slur
and drool, your brain's a ball of playdough squeezed

out the foramen magnum in just 40 minutes.
Watching your belly slowly expand, I'm showing through.

A slap. Now your blood and mine mingle differently.
Settled lividity into the recliner. Slippers housecoat

and a mug of tea. The TV left on, muted. I sat
on the adjacent couch, hot tea in hand.

Dreaming the triage nurse had become
very unprofessional, I woke up to your ears

boxed in my sleepy thighs. Your wife had begged
you not to go out. That night working untethered

you fell, head first. Two black eyes and face
elongated. Out in the open field, a first, a tiny

island atop shed t-shirts. The sea of clover
and bees. Your eyes reflecting August clouds.

A grandmother's cookbook diagram. Preparation
involved a twist of the middle fin, pull. Crayfish

we caught in the creek. Hara-kiri in the tub,
Your sandwich sliced wide, left unsampled.

Tipped off next of kin as they returned home.
Epsom seasoned, making waves in the clawfoot tub.

Osmosis absorbed, taking you in. Sopping up with towels.
A necessary errand done in heavy spring thunderstorm.

Irreversible pops of love-struck frogs under radials.
Walking home from the casino, loyalty card lanyard.

Unlucky is one struck by a driver having a heart attack. Careening.
Repeating on the radio, that they could

find you in a lethal arrhythmia lying beside a trailer
with "Hope for Life" across its side. Premeditated.

Strange to have set a time. Unable to make eye contact
with the vet upstairs. Naked in the cocoon of the living

room, where all the living had concluded. The matted
white dog beside you for days, would not eat.

A depression in you, and the roof. Breathing
shallow, dragging you to a more stable section.

Twenty-two stories later: rushing to the elevator
and out to the ambulance. Stop. A brief phone

call, then an awkward trip back upstairs
and into a still warm bed. Really it had happened

half way down the stairs. Your husband looking on
the dresser for Kleenex. White lies about it en route.

Second floor couch at the bar. Thirsty patrons downstairs
I should be tending, but your blue eyes were all.

Drunk in alcohol, splayed out pinned, cut out one
of your six-pack of testicles. Made a slide of your sperm.

That was the assignment. While you showered
for the funeral. I cut out the obit. Considered which magnet

words best to frame him with. Your awful, curled lips,
the door taped shut. Charcoal briquettes now extinguished

in the sink. Spelling your surname it surprised both of us.
A precordial thump reaction rhythm organized. Soon,

you talked again, just our bodies for language, us waiting
in the kitchen for your son to arrive. Your husband

on the floor upstairs, cold. Cramps and bleeding
while lifting a woman having a miscarriage.

The difference between us that day was her feigning.
That night uncooperative nerves prevent your rise.

So you watch me help myself instead. I think even more
of you. Crackles of aspiration. Blue limp hot potato ninety

days new. Do Not instructions. Conflicted mother holding
a tiny mask. An abruptly cancelled transfer of the neonatal

incubator and its team generally denotes a code pink
conclusion. You were the reason why I insist my husband

anchors every bookshelf, dresser and cabinet to the wall.
The belt you wear everyday was your father's staple.

The accident left the inner-side pocked with his bloodstains.
Stewing beef-like, tenderized by a baseball bat –

not that I would have recognized your face otherwise.
You finished the cigarette. Sent home three hours ago,

I doubted your claim of 200 pills, as you casually sauntered
to meet us. Too high, holding her daughter, calling

out 'momma'. The overdose easily reversible if you
had called before hiding the evidence. Under a duvet

on the couch, a leg cast recently set. Your two kids
'don't want mommy to be dead. I want her to make me chicken.'

I don't want mommy to be dead. I want her to make me chicken.

I don't want mommy to be dead. I want her to make me chicken.

I don't want mommy to be dead. I want her to make me chicken.

I don't want mommy to be dead. I want her to make me chicken.

I don't want mommy to be dead. I want her to make me chicken.

Unprecedented

CHRONOLOGY

A gamble, our pizza's ready in 10. My partner
retires in three months or thirty something
shifts. Last week the patient had a fever
or headache. We've been downtown five
hours now. Don a paper gown in the wind.
Knot secure the neck and waist, respirator next.
Wedge googles over glasses. Gloves over gown
wrist. Her mother deftly dicing onions for tonight.
Unfurl the stretcher/ reach under gown/lock up
curb/tight turns the ramp/elevator
down the hall. Hypoxic brain injury happens
within three to six minutes. The water is finally
hot enough as her whole body folds to meet
the drain. But first she takes a shower, to wake up
a little. These days of quarantine drag on.

ISOLATION ROOMS

1. March Break

Lightly to my children 'Darlings
you'll catch it for sure' knowing meanwhile
coworkers, each of them fathers, begin
to accommodate themselves, separate
work and loved ones. For a long haul
I'll go only as far as the basement, kids.
Take stock of nitrile gloves and respirators,
non-perishables. I am the most likely
vector, only half joking to neighbours.
There is exactly one day of school
between the morning announcement
and September. Hardly enough time to prepare
a will. 'Children get it, yes, mildly'. If more were
dying how differently would I carry on?

2. Exposure

How differently could I carry on
in the back of the ambulance? She follows
suit, reclines on the stretcher by request.
Her body radiates fever, hasn't been
tasting anything. An eight-year-old son
sits asymptomatically on the jump-seat.
Novel virus panic when we disclose ourselves
to hospital. Is this what the 80's were like?
Before triage, staff nervously demand I doff
down at the threshold. Ditch yellow gown,
gloves and N95. I apologize, escort them
myself. Medics like ghosts, move through
too many spaces. She arrived six days
ago on a plane from New York city.

3. Not all Things Being Equinox

Six days since transporting the New York
woman, no fevers here. Pandemics
aren't awful for everyone. Reassuring
my spouse with slow meals and elaborate cocktails.
Two weeks housebound paid. A record number
of days home together as a family.
"I don't have time" rendered invalid.
Face paint, forts, so many costumes!
Everyone else was tending sourdough starters,
but I used flour to craft a five-foot tall jackalope
from paper mâché. Teal with wild orange eyes.
Rebirth on our front porch, chocolate,
wily freedom. Easter morning snuck him out
beside the bike trail to surprise morning joggers.

4. Speakeasy

'Speaking Moistly' A surprise for morning viewers
as the ASL interpreter visibly shudders,
Words Trudeau immediately regrets. Mask
fashion this season's hottest trend.
Meanwhile, in healthcare we liberate
scrub cap style from surgeons, followed
up by beleaguered 'layers of PPE' selfies.
At night we get vulnerable, give each other
haircuts. Working to flatten the curve
with dog clippers at 2am. A departmental
speakeasy. This moonshine hand sanitizer
smells harsh-as narcissus staring at ourselves
on Zoom too long. Drown in information. Be
damned by paranoia disguised as knowing.

5. Hesitancy

Damned paranoia disguised as knowing
smacks of Lovecraftian cosmic horror.
Dear Uncle, hopefully in camp 'Wait and See'
rather than full Alt-Right. You text-plead
me to reconsider, or at least wait awhile,
on the vaccine. I counter, layman
the science. Frame mRNA as 'recipe cards.'
Express optimism about initiatives
in public health. You survived being out in the '80's
and a significant brain injury at work.
Your sequelae; anterograde and lost
filters. Voting against your own interests.
I'm still indebted for all your support. One
reason I get vaccinated is to protect you.

6. Role Identity

I get vaccinated to protect you.
Half-price takeout for heroes! Heroes?
The uniform mistaken for self. Now
basic femmes prevail. What the hell is
eyelash minking anyway? Science nerd who
lifts when gyms are open. Survives night shift.
Eats joy and germinates. Cheers! Embrace this
form. Volunteer serology. Titres of wild
caught versus acquired antibodies.
In hindsight, after a decade of exposure
my colostrum was probably the greatest gift.
"Love you mommy," "Miss you," "Need you mommy."
Son draws our family. Fruiting bodies show
not unlike mycelium we are all connected.

7. CareMongering-TO

Not unlike mycelium we are all connected.
This virtual supportive catch basin functions
as community resource. Folks express a need,
neighbours tender and fulfill. Fruit the foodbank
lacked. Birthday cake for a child. Rights regarding
renoviction. Handmade masks and pop-up clinics.
Benevolence delivered directly is beauty.
'Be More Kind'- spray painted bike path graffiti.
Attestation your need, and I'll catch myself
judging a post, or patient, requesting
accommodation. Reach beyond the typical
compassion scarcity. Language matters.
How quickly we replaced the term social
with physical in respect to distancing.

8. Bottle Half Empty

Physical replaced social in many respects.
The label reads Mountsberg. Half empty
bottle of maple syrup. I attempt to
ration the palpable evidence from last
time my dad visited. Sporadic before
lockdown. The sugarbush incorporates
a rehab centre -for raptors. Night owls
boiling off droplet precautions. Closeted
dependency. 'Tis the season again
though this time all twelve steps are cancelled.
Inviting a precarious isolation
not everyone is safe alone at home. He
won't return calls until he's sober next, but
he'll respond to a life-status check via text.

9. Apnea

At work, I often respond to life status checks.
Today, a bubble bath, novel open, personal
effects on a hotel room desk. Luxury as
a temporary pandemic measure. Still,
some prefer the autonomy of tents.
Paramedics 'should consider' withholding
manual ventilation. His friend tucks twenty
bucks in the stretcher sheet. Naloxone
first, a reversal of our standard practice.
He wakes up surprised and pleasant. Most
notably, hasn't been hurled into withdrawal.
"Maybe a little heroin?" Sheepishly grins.
Inadequate respirations inclusive. This
job's taught me everything is multifactorial.

10. Community Medicine

Everything is multifactorial on this job.
Social determinants of health overlay
COVID case distribution. Inconspicuous
barriers to care. At a ratio nearing 7:1
the city's budget favours emergency
services that might prioritize protection
of property ahead of life or limb.
Consider withholding breath as moral
injury. Breonna Taylor was a medic.
I'm working on my homework but I've also
driven my whiteness as a stretcher between
a racist and a young medic. Dismissed cops
from the back of an ambulance long before
those situations could go too far.

11. To the Poets

Before situations go too far, or perhaps
that's exactly when poets precipitate
experience. Compose an emotive
cellular response. Fragmentary language
crown attempts to wed the historical
record. Thucydides was not a poet
exiled in the thick of it, deemed no
longer essential. Caught the plague. Kept impartial.
Have you learned to smile with just your eyes yet?
despite this little rectangle song covering
your mouth. The pandemic is a constraint
in fourteen lines. I'll function as union steward
a woman, and a body of wage-labour,
remind everyone there's no visitors here.

12. No visitors

Remind everyone that there are no visitors
at this hospital or that one, few make
exceptions for translators these days. It's a choice
to die surrounded by family or medical
intervention, not both. A cool sip of water,
embrace. She delivers her last words
in person. No, take a moment. Either she comes
back or she won't. What would you do? They ask.
What makes a good death? It's very personal.
Consider a birth plan in reverse. At home
or in hospital? Pain control? Who attends?
What's changed is reversible strokes, cardiac stents,
antibiotics. What dying actually
looks like. Soon comes the day that everybody cries.

13. Inevitability

Today is the day everyone cries.
They had been careful for so long. Hoping
to avoid an ambulance ride. This leg's
visible shortening and external
rotation claims otherwise. Indignant
glassy eyes at the nursing home
he's already positive. Wife can't
tend to him here or there. Careful
so careful, suspicious of us broaching
an emotional threshold. Uncommon vectors
in steel toes. Denying accompaniment
by their own children. Prompt a proper
goodbye. Remember to bring a phone, a charger.
What exactly am I doing for a living?

14. To the Beloved

"Do you know what I do for a living?" I ask
again. He answers: we've got it better than
most. Domestic proximity. I've never cared
much for flipping records have I? Could I just
sleep for 12 hours? A joint, some wine, a show
on the couch? House in constant disaster.
It'll get better after this 'unprecedented'
strain. What should I write into a love poem
addressed to you? Eye roll. Maybe I could
reference Cohen's 'Hallelujah'? The 4th, the 5th
time we cut each other's hair in the kitchen.
About how we're kind of broken,
That this is no celebratory march? End it lightly,
with a 'my darling, you'll catch it for sure.'

IT'S HARD NOT TO SLAM A FIST ON THE TABLE WHEN THE FINISH LINE KEEPS LURCHING FURTHER AHEAD- OR- THIRD WAVE

"Maybe you were a mother. It was possible. Maybe you were dead. There are ways to be both"

-Shira Erlichman

No   Sir, take a moment   to say goodbye   to your mother   you
understand   there are   only two   absolutely   no visitors   out-
come   in hospital   I'll be in the hall   take a minute   please   he's
mastered   mute   unmute and   refreshing the page   at six years
old   family quarantine   round three   no tail end   of lounge wear
or feral toddler   sussing out the cupboards   badly hidden   wrappers
in the couch   damn sneaky raccoons   days of screen time   dubious
exposure   the man   screened   negative   eye protection   only re-
quired   for failed   screenings   goggles overtop prescription   glasses
always fogging   rivulets   looks silence   despondence   en route the
trauma centre   one drink   too many   step ladder slipped   affix-
ing   failed is insensitive   the noose   a positive   household contact
noted in the sending documents   I had secured   his stretcher straps
just prior   I had secured   concert tickets   no   a vaccine ap-
pointment   for the next day   it had only taken   three hours   of
constant   refreshing   on my phone screen   I had to cancel   and
isolate   teach   the six year old   still life practice   in pastels
call my dad   the most self-aware   alcoholism   I'm worried about
his   isolation   despite the bodies   filling up   refrigerated
transport trucks   in the forest city   he's full of guilt   grown of
absence   my learned   foresight   to buy a couple   extra presence
for my kids   write his name   he listens   hesitates   to dis-
close much   some weeks   but always calls   often asks   how
I'm   getting along   with my spouse   confesses to him   my
husband that is   one night over drinks   how he regrets leaving
my mom   my mom   hesitates   about   the vaccine   despite
working in a hospital   and chronic bronchitis   grade one teacher
scolds intermittently   through floor boards   the youngest child

finally   into outdoor preschool   this is   respite care   two days
a week   they tried   to skip over us   because   my job   a per-
ceived risk   to the cohort   I called them   out on it   I need
this   he comes home   smelling   of homemade   beef
barley soup   paints with beet juice   North American doctors   may
soon   make decisions   based on   resource scarcity   now let
us introduce   the term   moral injury   your cake   is illegal
the co-worker hissed   get fucked   so is the twelve of us   in this
room   using common dishes   hand washed in Dawn   dou-
ble-think is   essential work   this other woman is   ninety-six
years old   speaks only Russian   what would you do?   her
family asks   there are   no visitors   my chorus refrain   a chance
she could die   at home   surrounded by family   or   she can
come with us   to hospital   a year ago   there would have been
no question   on their part   the full toll   would consider   the
backlog   of surgeries   imaging   those who will   certainly die
of previously   treatable   also   so many seniors   too afraid
to call us   disease vectors   to our faces   to invite us over
their threshold   too afraid   of the hospital   right now
choosing death   instead   of stents   this woman   had the most
advanced   breast cancer   I've ever   hard purple   bleeding
orange peel   how big was it   first lockdown ?   a thumbnail
she stays   invites her family   for Easter   next Sunday   it's still
much too soon   to consider   the pandemic   positively impacting
our concept of   death care   not framed as   medical failure   pal-
liation   at home   the idea of   a good death   is an essay   I've
been trying to write   forever   but I sleep   a lot   now   may-
be   too much   on spouses birthday   after I shuck   a few
bivalves   make elaborate   quarantini's   we argue intensely
I catch a glimpse of terror   desperation   I've not seen before
now realize   he needs   reassurance   is not unworthy   of love
despite   adulterous   past lovers   a complicated backstory
with his mother   depression   I have never   understood

women who choose   a man   over their children   he cannot
comprehend   out-sourcing   physical affection   or sex   de-
spite my offering up   a hall-pass   he's a monogamist   at heart
which isn't   a bad thing   but you should   anticipate   drought
conditions   with young children   years of working   opposites
I am acutely   out of my body   no visitors please   I have been   the
eldest son states   the worst part about this   family   is that
we are all heartbroken   September is coming   they'll both   be
in school   will it be easier then?   I believe   in quieter   should
be cherishing   this time   I'm told   they grow so fast   the
crafts and costumes   epoch   of the pandemic   ended months
ago   children are   an indicator species   of a community   did
you know   biologists have   observed that   urban squirrels
regularly consume meat   are terrible at   caching   my son asks
my mother-in-law   about a sleepover   a weekend sometime
since mom and dad   are fighting   a lot   she just   changed
the subject   cookie anyone?   does not subscribe   to the grand-
mother hypothesis   a parabolic   rise of cases   domestic
and   child abuse   I witness   this fallout   young families
no support   no visitors   equals no help   caremongering   over-
whelmed   lack of resource   shaking yes   evisceration   more
than once   defense wounds   on a four year old   do you know what
I do for a living?   I ask him again   and then   cherry on top   my
near-immortal   grandfather   moves in with my uncles   elim-
inating   the only source   of help   we had   I wake up   from
nightshift   gobble   six pieces of   buttered cinnamon toast
and a cold   medium rare   lamb chop   time gets skewered   so
often   I ask people   to measure   seizures   in punk songs   *I*
Wanna Be Sedated   is 2 minutes 19seconds   it's been   three weeks
or so   I guess I'm due for him   to bring up   divorce again
I love   herding dogs   so smart   yes   but more so
keen   body language   readers   probably   didn't need a pup-
py   to the overwhelm   right now   though   I'll give him
that one   a guaranteed hour   almost alone   every day   the
layers of   noise   not loud   necessarily   but ingratiating
boils up   something   cortisol probably   what I wouldn't do

for some silence   which is   apparently a construct   of the hearing
but it   sublimates   into anger   anyhow   I've got   a low
snarl   and some deep   shame   how often   I've been yelling
at my kids   over nothing   it's the opposite   of skin hunger
weighty layers   of   sound and presence   the other mothers
whisper   same here   when the oldest son   starts   compul-
sively   washing his hands   twice through   the alphabet   ev-
ery time   is distressed at   interruption   is washing again
after touching   his own face   at home   again after holding
almost anything   tries to use elbows instead   washes again   ev-
ery   ten to twenty minutes   until his hands   turn red and bleed
clinical   so hard   to get my   worries out   as anything   but
stern   instead of   compassion   a crisp   and skeletal
pothos   hangs from the skylight   dead since December   it's not
alone   looks like it's   takeout again tonight   a more virulent
strain   begins to dominate but I can't maintain   any panic   this
long   getting laissez faire   about the yellow gowns   but my
spouse   still can't get   a vaccine   the children   get sore throats
trouble swallowing   fever   and curiously red eyes   however
they are experienced   in negotiating   their swab-bribe price   false
alarm   only costs me   a cake-pop   and pokèmon cards   another
virus   that   forever   lives in my   face   nests in the   tri-
geminal nerve   only shows up   under extreme   physiologic
stress   normally   only every couple years   or so   keeps
trying   to turn   my lips and eyelids   whole face   on occasion
into swaths   of weeping   blisters   the antivirals   not entire-
ly effective   this time   household   strata of debris   laundry
on underused furniture   another aspect of   no visitor refrain   silt
up   accumulation   on shift   I keep entering   other people's
homes   now the whole family   gets sick   by degrees
which is new   actually   people feel   awful   still have to
care   for others   there is no one   else   we checked   vi-
tals   oxygen saturation mainly   we can   take her alone   no
visitor refrain   doesn't need oxygen   they send her back   by
cab   more contacts   call back   when she starts   working
harder   to breath   triage often   discharges   directly   from

stretcher   the coroner   issues   death certificates   a statement
now   these people   we often   assessed   suddenly dying
hours later   a lot to shoulder   liability   our function   is
not   should never be   gatekeepers   of health care   we are
awaiting   medical direction   a directive   it is never   enacted
despite a field hospital   erected   adjacent   our hospital   there
is   no one left   to staff it   in a dream   I schedule   my own
medically assisted   death   casually as   a dentist appointment
somewhere   between six   and seventeen   times a day   I
receive a text   for available   overtime shifts   it asks me to reply
'read'   so I pick up   a book   instead   unless   it's a
vaccine clinic   one that   doesn't have   plexiglass   or has cut
cotton balls   in half   but won't   turn you away   for no   health
card   should have several   translators   and   speakers   blaring
music   for the line-up   around the block   because   an
appointment   is a barrier   other times   a public health nurse
and myself   in a spare bedroom   of a rooming house   these
days   the most   positive   I've had   in months   great
COVID denier   filter   everyone wears a mask   properly   even
my spouse   gets jabbed   my mother quits   her hospital job
instead   my son   is assigned   a project   on community
helpers   he chooses   parks and rec   he asks if there   are
any courses   I could take   to be a   better mom?   In May
spouse and I   bristle   a record length of time   apathetic
Mother's Day   the youngest   gifts me a stone   a bit   rough
but   a good weight   thick thighs   save lives   I request
Feist's Metals   on the turntable   oh   the we're fighting   record
he says   makes some   excellent waffles   in spite of it   in-
sert   elder millennial   laugh-cry emojis   and side parts
here   I propose   framing   an apartment door   to
the   basement   he offers   to not work   every day   I'm
off   making it   impossible   to save   first and last   a
well-meaning   friend   asks if   I wouldn't have   preferred
a situation   where I could be   home   making art   I'm
no good at   stay-at-home   I love   my family   more
with some space   my own mother   shows up   two hours late

for the overpriced   local brunch   besides   I could never
accept   that amount   of vulnerability   speaking of   my
dad   comes for the weekend   he and my husband   sound-
proof   and vapour barrier   the shed   into a studio   qui-
et   with a deadlock   of one's own   no visitors refrain   he calls it
my   habitat   the neighbours kid   makes   a COVID piña-
ta   red paper   spike proteins   aerosolized   candy   case
counts   plummeting   I watch   a beautiful man   roller-
blading though   an abandoned   financial district   no out of
town   visitors   at midnight   gracefully   he jumps and spins
fully   in his body   and   I try   care-giving   again

OMICRON GRAND FINALE

Enacted
Auxiliary Medical Directive
                    by now   you'd expect me to share

inevitability
n-caspid antibodies, my serology

                    claims otherwise (I'm as surprised as you)

droplet precautions nowadays   asymptomatic
        laminated placards   wildcards
                          randomized
above hallway stretchers

MEDIC   "Are you vaccinated?"
MAN WITH MINOR COMPLAINT "Do you think I'm stupid?"
MEDIC   "Do you have a better mask
                                for the waiting room?"

            the service issues
            rapid test boxes of 25
not unlike tampons it's really all about the insertion angle

occasional instability or deep neck pain
                    ...smacks of   freedom

don't forget context   from
                    in poetry
                    in   paramedicine

practice postures of defeat   managing capacity.

(my retired medic neighbour
brandishes two new knees)

Authorized by Base Hospital

are heart opening poses currently encouraged or contraindicated?

to treat and release

on the third attempt
I finally secure

spicy garlic pork ramen

it's a marathon   been carb-loading for two years

CODE BLUE's   overhead   all   the   time

which aspect am I?

fertile hips or

in the truck eating pomegranate arils scowling at January
body's in the house   coroner's in my contacts

(Fleet Foxes *White Winter Hymnal*)

accumulated snow sirens muffed

ACCLAIMED POET "Some years the ambulances
seem louder"

percepticide

on the billboard   "A peptide to prevent PTSD"

    we wouldn't survive if we remembered everything (laughs)

trauma returns
in reaction
not memory

                    transition to endemic
                    each night the youngest
"cuddle me mommy"
      I'll always be their first   exposure

DISCLAIMER

The views, thoughts and opinions expressed in this collection of poetry are solely those of the author and do not reflect the opinions, lived experiences, beliefs or practices of other paramedics, the Corporation of the City of Toronto, Toronto Paramedic Services, Sunnybrook Base Hospital Group, or the Ontario Ministry of Health.

There are many instances of found text incorporated into the following poems. They are most certainly used outside of their intended context.

NOTES

These poems were written during the later half of my fifteen years as a Paramedic in a large urban service. While events and likenesses are based in reality no patients are identifiable as per PHIPA standards. Fellow medics and non-patients featured were made aware of their poetic cameos that might be read by the 75 or so anticipated readers of this book.

For context, paramedics are nearly feral and the least popular of the three Emergency services in both media visibility and toy production, though we have the darkest sense of humour. When we are able to gather together the topic almost invariably steers towards a particular style of anecdotal story sharing where the most noteworthy and unbelievable calls are retold. This is also known as trauma-bonding.

In Ontario paramedics are employed by a municipality and not a specific hospital, so we are not confined to a particular response area, and can end up quite far from our 'home' station in 12 hours. Some paramedics are very good at meal prepping for a set of shifts. I am not one of those medics. When I end up in an unfamiliar part of the city I try to make the best of it by relishing novel take-out options. I also just enjoy eating the variety of food available in such a diverse city, so, food is featured frequently in my poems.

PREFACE TO BASIC LIFE SUPPORT—Utilizes phrases from the Preface to BLS Patient Care Standards 2.0.

PRONOUNCED/WORKABLE—Categorizes the two types of Vital Signs Absent bodies.

10-8—Incorporates parts of Toronto Paramedic Sercvice S.O.P about proceeding through red lights, and a Geocode reference to my first Toronto apartment.

10-7—Utilizes phrases from the Ambulance Act, and an entry on 'CPR in Adults' from Web MD

ANCEDOTAL—Utilizes a line from a translated Kim Hyesoon poem. 'Locards theory' is a central tenant in Forensic Science. 'Mother, Jugs and Speed' is a 1976 dark comedy film in which Bill Cosby is the least sexually inappropriate character.

OUT OF SERVICE—Is in the form of a glosa, and utilizing four lines from Emily Dickenson's 1852 'Valentine to William Howland' and also references an Aviation Safety report following the death of Paramedic/Helicopter pilot/stuntman Anton Tyukodi.

WORK-WIFE—Utilizes phrases from a journal article that my former work partner co-authored 'Paramedics Experiences with Death Notification: A Qualitative Study' as well as numerous personal text messages and inside jokes.

THE LAY-HERO ARCHETYPE AND THE PUBLIC ACCESS DEFIBRILLATOR—Uses phrases from a journal article 'A Grounded Theory Study of Bystander CPR', Alice Notley's 'The Descent of Alette' and an article on 'The Archetypal Hero in Literature, Religion, Movies and Pop Culture'

PANTOUM—The internet meme with the dog and cup of coffee in the flaming room seemed very pertinent.

10-9—Uses a few lines from the Highway Traffic Act and a Wikipedia entry on 'Wolf-Parkison-White Syndrome'. 'Wages for Tenderness' was spray painted graffiti on a building near Queen and Bathurst.

B IS FOR BASIC LIFE SUPPORT—Incorporates some phrases from a journal article titled 'Role Identity, Dissonance, and Distress among Paramedics', and a nearly immediately retracted letter from the then-deputy-chief likening the customer service aspect of prehospital care to making cheeseburgers. Also, a nod to the 1999 Martin Scorsese film 'Bringing Out the Dead' where Nicholas Cage plays a burnt-out NYC medic.

CIMEX LECTULARIS—Uses some language from a Wikipedia article on Bedbugs. The 'Seduce Me!' quote is from the Isabella Rossellini series of "Green Porno' shorts.

CEREBROVASCULAR ACCIDENT—Utilizes some language from Sunnybrook's 'Paramedic Care Guide 3.3.1', and the BLS Patient Care Standards 2.0. There is also a quote from a children's book "Have you Seen My Dragon" given to my kids by my uncle, who also uttered the quote about pruning the tables.

DESTINATION—Excerpt taken from an interview in Now Magazine with ANSER the Toronto based graffiti artist. Toronto East General Hospital was renamed Michael Garron Hospital after receiving a 50-million-dollar donation by the late child's parents.

LEISURE WORLD—From a dry-erase board on a dementia care floor in a nursing home.

SUBPOENA— Questions from the defence attorney

MAJOR INCIDENT FIELD GUIDE—Some language used from the 'Summary of the Final Report on the Truth and Reconciliation Commission of Canada' as well as the 'Emergency Response Guidebook 2016' copies of which are placed in each Toronto ambulance.

GOOGLE TRANSLATE APP HISTORY—This is how the translations appeared in the phone application. I cannot speak to how inaccurate these translations might actually be.

HOTEL SIERRA—Is constructed entirely from found text. Four sources were used, A Toronto Paramedic Service S.O.P. titled 'Hotel Sierra', an S.O.P. on 'Professional Appearance', the 'Occupational Health and Safety Act, and the CUPE Collective Agreement 2010.

UN-BARREN NEWLY—Some text taken from a personal ultrasound report. Scarborough Grace Hospital. September 2012

CONTEMPORARY PSYCHOPOMP—Utilizes some phrases from the journal articles 'Role Identity, Dissonance, and Distress Among Paramedics' and 'A Grounded Theory Study of Bystander CPR' as well as a nod to the CBC National Research Council Time Signal.

BLS STANDARDS- OBSTETRICS—Uses phrases from BLS 2.0.

WAIVER- Some language from the Personal Health Information Privacy

Act, as well as text from personal transcripts of Midwife and Obstetrician discharge documents.

WORK HARDENING—Is the term given to the 3-5 shifts when a paramedic returns to work after any leave of more than 3 months. Inspired by the long poem 'Alphabet' by Inger Christensen, and the Fibonacci sequence 0,1,1,2,3,5,8,13....377....

BLS STANDARDS- PEDIATRIC GENERAL ASSESSMENT—Uses phrases from BLS Patient Care Standards 2.0 on alternate lines.

DRIVERS—That 'This is Fine...' meme surfaces again.

14.TO THE BELOVED—References Leonard Cohen's 'Hallelujah'.

THIRD WAVE—The inspiration for this long form is from Alice Notley's 'The Descent of Alette' and Victoria Chang's 'I am a Miner. The Light Burns Blue'

OMICRON GRAND FINALE—Acclaimed Poet is...

ACKNOWLEDGMENTS

Gratitude to the editors of the literary journals and small presses who previously published some of these poems in print and online: Arc, CV2, Grain, BAD NUDES, Feathertale.com, Meat for Tea, Vallum and Frog Hollow Press.

Forever indebted to Hoa Nguyen for her mentorship and guidance during my MFA, as well as her homebased workshop series, where the earliest versions of some of these poems germinated in 2017.

Recognition to Shane Neilson as another significant mentor. Thank you for all the advice, edits and opportunities. Similar thanks to the Jeremy Luke Hill (the other half of Gordon Hill Press) for all of the local literary community building and event opportunities.

Grateful to the well-respected Canadian poets who have also laid eyes and offered up suggestions on some of these poems: Madhur Anand, Dionne Brand and Susan Holbrook.

Thank you to Jim Johnstone for the final edits and Denis De Klerck for the opportunity to publish this collection.

Acknowledgment to the University of Guelph Creative Writing MFA Program – Class of 2022 instructors and classmates for their support and influence. Also, thanks to the Banff Centre Spring Writers Retreat (Spring 2022) for the time to focus solely on this project – even if via online.

Thank you to the poetry and small press communities in Guelph and Toronto. For the events, the community building and Zine fair field trips. Especially those at PSGuelph.

To LeeAnne Douglas, Jeff Sobil, Sekar Vupputuri and Kenneth Ng as my paramedic work-spouses of the last decade. To Justin Mausz for sending me pre-publication copies of his paramedic themed research articles to turn into poetry fodder. To the rest of my trauma bonded Toronto EMS family.

To my family: Mom, Dad, Uncle Robb, Uncle Carl and the many, many others. To Steve- who puts up with, and more often embraces the shift work, the chaos, the fur and the syrup on the home front.

Forever grateful to learn and grow with Roenigk and Jonas.

Thank you.

Candace de Taeye's poetry has been previously published in *Arc, BAD NUDES, Carousel, CNQ, CV2, Grain, Vallum* and others. She very recently completed an MFA in Creative Writing from the University of Guelph. She has published two chapbooks 'Roe' and 'The Ambulance Act'. During the day, and more often at night she works as a paramedic in Toronto's downtown core. She lives in Guelph with her partner, kids, some geriatric treefrogs and a 25 lb tortoise.